Discovering Our Heritage
A Cultural Explorer's Toolkit

Table of Contents

Culture is the widening of the mind and of the spirit.

— Jawaharlal Nehru

Chapter 1. Introduction

Immerse yourself in a grand tapestry of human experience as we unravel the many threads that make up our global community in this Special Report, "Discovering Our Heritage: A Cultural Explorer's Toolkit". Let's set sail on a vibrant journey through time and drop anchor in fascinating corners of our shared past. As we delve into the vibrant, multi-cultural pageantry of human history, each colourful tradition, captivating folk tale, and priceless artifact takes on a deeper meaning, all uniquely contributing to the world's shared heritage. This isn't just a guide. It's an invitation to broaden your horizons, to understand our intertwined pasts better and appreciate the diverse cultures that enrich our world today. Come, be a part of this promising exploration that could change how you view our world. Bring out the cultural explorer in you, stoke your curiosity, and evoke a sense of wonder. By purchasing this Special Report, you get more than just a book, you open up a world of discovery!

Chapter 2. Unlocking the Mysteries of our Ancestors

In our collective quest to comprehend the enigmatic panorama of human history, we set out on the first leg of our journey: drawing back the veil of antiquity to expose the fascinating mysteries of our ancestors whose life and times played a pivotal role in the shaping of human existence as we know it today.

2.1. Encountering the First Humans

In exploring our ancient history, we unearth our beginnings with the first humans, Homo Sapiens. Evidence points to their emergence in Africa approximately 200,000 years ago, marking a fundamental shift in the evolution of life on Earth. Our understanding of these first humans is primarily drawn from the study of archeological remnants – bone fragments, tools, and other artifacts they left behind. Fossils provide a tangible link to our primordial past and offer a sobering testament to our intricate journey from primitive forms to complex beings.

2.2. Understanding Primitive Societies

As we delve deeper into primitive societies, we see the shift from solitary survivalists to community builders. Human settlements, using rudimentary technologies, began to spring up around fertile lands and water bodies, leading to the genesis of the first agrarian cultures. These societies, underpinned by shared beliefs, collective labor, basic rule systems, and interdependence, were the predecessor to the structured societies we reside in today. In these basic communities, we can trace the roots of today's complex economic and civic structures.

2.3. Advancements and Discoveries

Advancements in technology and the human capacity for discovery were hallmark characteristics of our ancestors. Delving into their innovative spirit, we find remarkable firsts. The creation of tools rendered from wood and stone transformed homo sapiens' interaction with their environment. Fire's discovery, consistently heralded as one of humanity's greatest breakthroughs, not only provided warmth and protection but revolutionized food consumption, leading to significant nutritional and communal benefits. The advent of language, while impossible to pin down to a precise moment, facilitated complex social structures and enabled the sharing of knowledge across generations.

2.4. Tracing Cultural Origins

From cave paintings to rudimentary forms of music and dance, early humans engaged in the creation and appreciation of expressive and communicative art forms. These primeval expressions of creativity are the foundation of our rich and diverse cultural tapestry today. Each community's unique interpretations of these forms honor their individual journeys and shared experiences.

2.5. Genealogy and Anthropology

Human genealogy and anthropology become central in decoding the mysteries of our ancestors. By studying human genetics, anthropologists can trace human lineages back to ancient times, revealing a fascinating web of interconnections. This science robustly reveals the migration patterns of our forebears, highlighting how extensively early humans colonized the globe.

2.6. Formation of Civilizations

The formation of civilizations and the rise of the empires represents a significant phase in our ancestral journey. The emergence of structured political, religious, and economic systems fundamentally transformed human society. These ancient civilizations gave birth to remarkable architectural feats, innovative agricultural practices, groundbreaking philosophical ideas, and the refinement of written language.

2.7. Conclusion

Exploring these historical threads provides a revealing glimpse into the collective journey of humanity. The challenges faced and overcome, the ingenuity exhibited, the collective experiences shared, all paint a riveting portrait of our ancestors. Through this understanding, we not only appreciate the complexity of our past but also comprehend the trajectory of our future. Drawing closer to our roots, we grow increasingly cognizant of the ways in which their legacy lives on in the society we are, the lives we lead, and the world we inhabit today.

Chapter 3. Reading Cultural Landscapes: A Guide

Landscapes are an enigmatic entity, embodying the cumulative effects of nature and human activity. They showcase a region's cultural and historical evolution, transforming otherwise mundane spaces into compelling narratives that bare their soul and sing the symphony of their people. It behooves us, then, as seekers and learners, to understand how to unlock their profound secrets; how to "read" them in order to better comprehend the life histories pulsating within their confines.

3.1. The Art and Science of Reading Landscape

Outdoor spaces portray a detailed record of human interaction with the environment just waiting to be decoded. They act as snapshots of bygone eras, providing invaluable perspectives on historical, sociological, and cultural developments. This skill—the ability to "read" landscapes—is an art of observation, an exercise in deep listening, and a profound manifestation of the human yearning to comprehend our collective inheritance.

For cultural explorers, landscapes provide a textured canvas rich with embedded clues about the customs, ideals, and preferences of our predecessors. They reveal much about the area's environmental factors, societal norms, agricultural practices, trade routes, and architectural styles which have evolved over time. By learning to comprehend this intricate tapestry, you can glean vivid insights into the history of civilizations and penetrate the core essence of tangible human heritage etched onto the fabric of the world.

3.2. Tools to Decipher the Landscape

Like any good miner, the cultural prospector needs tools, methods, and perspectives to pry open the historical layering of landscapes, peek into its deep strata, and interpret the tales it whispers. The following approaches can help you reap rich dividends.

1. **Historic Maps and Documents**: Historical maps are a treasure trove for understanding the transformation of a landscape over time. They offer a glimpse of land use patterns, geographical features, and human settlements of the past. Similarly, historical documents provide context to the changes within a landscape. They can help you correlate transformations in the landscape with milestone events in a region's history.

2. **Archaeological Evidence**: Artifacts, monuments, and ruins provide hard evidence of human impact on the landscape. They are pointers to technological advances, social hierarchies, and shifts in cultural practices.

3. **Ethnography**: Understanding local folklore, myths, and indigenous knowledge can offer vital clues about landscape use and management. These oral histories and ethnographies provide an authentic lens to view the landscape from the perspective of the people who inhabited it.

4. **Field Survey**: Observing the visible features, such as field patterns, building styles, road layouts, and water systems, can help trace the chronology of development.Additionally, studying natural elements—such as flora and fauna indigenous to the region—can yield insights about the region's climatic history and land use choices made by its inhabitants.

3.3. Reading Landscape to Understand Social History

The patchwork fields, winding roads, quaint cottages, urban sprawl, or the abandoned mills in any landscape tell tales of the pulse of its people—their struggles and triumphs, their ingenuity and tradition, their adaptation and resistance.

For instance, consider the sunken lanes or 'hollow ways' of Europe. These tell a story of centuries of foot, cart, and livestock traffic wearing down the land. Or consider the layout of a medieval city—its fortified walls, narrow lanes, and central markets tell much about the security concerns, social fabric, and economic dynamics of the time.

Each element of the landscape thus acts as a testament of social history. In landscape reading, you stitch together these diverse clues to form a cohesive understanding of communal living through ages and to trace the influence of societal structures and processes on space creation and utilization.

3.4. Towards a Holistic Understanding of Cultural Landsccape

In conclusion, reading a cultural landscape isn't merely an intellectual pursuit. It's a path to a richer understanding of the continuum of human endeavor. It gives us clearer insights into our shared heritage, allowing us to appreciate the diversity of human experience.

Landscapes, thus understood, become much more than mere scenery. They stand as monumental, living museums of cultural memory, continually shaped by the ongoing drama of human existence.

Deciphering them equips us with a panoramic lens that captures the course of cultural evolution etched across the globe.

So, next time you venture into the open, remember that each building, road, or field is an artifact in itself—narrating histories, carrying the legacy of a culture, and inviting you to interact with it in an infinitely meaningful manner. With this understanding, you won't just traverse the landscape; you'll engage with it, read it, feel it, and comprehend the symphony of human culture.

Chapter 4. The Story in Symbols: Decoding Art and Architecture

The labyrinthine passageways of symbolism open a window into the collective human experience. By exploring the various symbols in art and architecture, we unlock a treasure trove of shared knowledge, opening up narratives that transcend borders and breach the walls of time.

4.1. The Power of Symbols in Art and Architecture

Symbols, in their essence, function as visual shorthand, compactly expressing multifaceted and often complex ideas within small, well-defined boundaries. Their omnipresence in every culture underscores their profound impact on human comprehension and social cohesion. In art and architecture, they establish a silent dialogue between the creator and the observer, nurturing an ongoing exchange of ideas and perceptions.

Ancient cave paintings, for example, yield a rich palette of symbols, depicting everything from hunting scenes and celestial bodies to abstract patterns and mythical beasts. These art pieces act as primal history books, painting a rich tableau of our ancestors' lives, their belief systems, and their understanding of the world around them.

4.2. Gleaning Insight from Iconic Architecture

The architectural marvels gracing our world, both past and present, stand as physical embodiments of human imagination, industry, and cultural ethos. Each monument is a testament to the builders' technical prowess and a reflection of the society's prevailing ideologies. They encode a broad spectrum of messages, from pure aesthetic enjoyment to political assertion, religious symbolism, social order, and cosmological beliefs.

Take, for example, the pyramids of Egypt, these grandiose edifices symbolize the pharaohs' eternal life and their divine connection. Similarly, the towering gothic cathedrals of medieval Europe prominently feature intricate symbolism in their architectural design. The verticality of these structures, reaching skyward, embodies humanity's spiritual aspiration and proximity to divinity.

4.3. The Art of Decoding Symbolism

Decoding the symbolism in art and architecture is akin to acquiring a new language. It invites us to view familiar scenes with fresh eyes and perceive subtleties that would otherwise fly below our radar. The art of reading symbols entails adopting an analytical mindset while maintaining an appreciation for aesthetics and conceptual potency.

As a starting point, it's often helpful to hone in on recurrent symbols and patterns. Common symbols span the gamut from animals, plants, mythological creatures, and geometric shapes to human figures and celestial bodies. Each of these symbols holds specific connotations, influenced by cultural contexts and historical eras.

4.4. Familiar Symbols and their Meanings

Perhaps no symbol is as universal as the circle. Often emblematic of unity, completeness, or the cyclical nature of life, it's found its way into the sacred geometry of various cultures, visible in religious motifs, architecture, and art. Another widely recognized symbol, the triangle, connotes stability and divine connectivity among myriad other interpretations.

In Asia, the dragon often stands for power, strength, and good luck. In contrast, Western cultures have historically viewed dragons as threatening creatures, denoting chaos or evil. These opposing interpretations highlight the critical role of cultural context in decoding symbols.

4.5. Symbol as a Societal Mirror

To delve into the symbology is to embark on a rich and rewarding journey to the depths of shared human experience. In decoding the symbols enshrined in art and architecture, we introduce ourselves to a complex network of narratives. These captivating stories, veiled in abstraction and smartly cloaked in geometry, are not just insightful but are also revelatory. They reflect the societies they sprang from, showing their history, their inspirations, their fears, and their hopes for the future.

This exploration is a testament to our shared heritage, a celebration of human creativity, and a realization of our interconnectedness. So let us proceed with a keen eye and an open mind, letting the symbols guide us through the annals of human history as we chart our journey forward.

Beyond the realm of this chapter, the entire book 'Discovering Our Heritage: A Cultural Explorer's Toolkit' encourages you to embark on more adventures, further igniting your curiosity about the world's rich tapestry of cultures. Happy exploring!

Chapter 5. The Language of Dance and Music in Cultural Expression

Dance and music have been an essential part of human existence since time immemorial. They are cultural threads weaving through the fabric of our history, helping us express our deepest emotions, celebrate our most significant moments, and communicate our most profound thoughts. Different cultures have honed unique art forms, expressions, rhythms, and movements that make dance and music its universal language. To fully appreciate the immense richness embedded in these cultural expressions, we need to delve deeper into their significance, scope and diversity, evolution over time, and the intricate ways they mirror societal realities.

5.1. The Significance and Scope of Dance and Music

Music and dance are integral to every culture's fabric, providing a vibrant lifeline to our shared human experience. People do more than merely listen to music or watch a dance; they feel it. It has the power to stand alone or be combined with other forms of art to tell a story or express an emotion. Music and dance can be a powerful vehicle for personal and communal expression, reflecting the Zeitgeist of the era or a specific community's mood.

Every culture manifests its unique rhythm and melodies, highlighting a rich variety of musical flavors. From the poignant operas of Italy and the hypnotic dance dramas of Thailand, to the rustic bluesy tunes of southern US and the lively jigs of Ireland – every culture presents a different blend of musical and dance expressions. Even within regions, there are subcultures with unique traditions, encapsulating a variety of emotions and experiences, representative of the socio-cultural milieu they are born out of.

From the haunting rhythms of a Gregorian chant to the exhilarating beat of African drum circles; from the serene elegance of the Japanese Noh dance to the exuberant frenzy of a Brazilian samba - these cultural expressions know no boundaries yet encapsulate the boundaries of the societies that birthed them.

5.2. Evolution of Dance and Music Over Time

Observing the evolution of dance and music provides a fascinating insight into how societies, people, and cultures evolve. Greek orchestras transitioned over centuries from the primal instinct of a communal beat to the sophisticated compositions we appreciate today. Similarly, dances have morphed from simple communal circles to intricate ballet sequences and beyond, adapting to societal changes, technological advancements, and shifts in thinking.

Imperial courts of China trademarked the complex dances during the Tang dynasty, reflecting the sophistication and refinement associated with the era. As societies changed, so did these dances, becoming more or less restrained, meshing with other forms of dance and accommodating changing societal norms. The technology played a significant part too. With the advent of recording technology in the 20th Century, music became more accessible, enabled mixing of styles, and caused a cultural cross-pollination that birthed genres like Jazz, Rock n' Roll and Hip Hop.

5.3. Dance and Music: Mirrors to Society

Dance and music transcend being mere mediums of entertainment. They are rich repositories of historical context, societal values, and communal memory. The lyrics of folk songs often carry tales of local heroes, mythical creatures, historical battles, and everyday life, offering a panoramic view of the culture. Dance forms like Bharatanatyam from Southern India, encapsulate centuries of religious and philosophical narratives, while dances like the Waltz carry in them the stories of courtly manners and etiquette.

The protest songs of the 1960s told tales of civil rights strife and anti-war sentiment, while the rise of hip-hop in marginalized communities in the US during the 80s and 90s was a form of resistance art, expressing discontent about societal issues. Dance, too, was not far behind. The evolution of breakdancing, for instance, was a move towards democratizing dance, moving away from elitist ballet to street corners and clubs.

5.4. Embracing the Language of Dance and Music Across Cultures

To truly appreciate the language of dance and music across different cultures, it is essential to engage and participate actively. Attend local performances, support indigenous artists, learn an instrument, or immerse yourself in a dance form. Only through active engagement can one understand the depth and breadth of these cultural expressions and their true magnificence.

Remember: Embracing this language is not about appropriation, but about understanding, appreciation, and respect. Everyone has a role to play in preserving these beautiful expressions and ensuring that they continue to enrich our lives for centuries to come.

In conclusion, dance and music serve as fascinating doors to understanding our shared human history and cultural diversity. By investing time and effort in comprehending these forms, we can foster mutual respect, bridging gaps across cultures. They really are the world's common language - a testament to our shared human experiences and the incredible diversity that makes us unique. As a cultural explorer, let's harness the power of this language to shape a more understanding, inclusive world.

Chapter 6. Foods and Feasts: Culinary Traditions Around the World

Diving headfirst into the gastronomic world, this chapter aims to inspire your culinary curiosity and engage your senses as we explore the rich tapestry of global culinary art; defined as much by the preparation methods and ingredients, as by the history, culture and geography of their places of origin. You will find each cuisine has a story to tell, each dish is a historian, chronicling triumphs, adversities, and of course, everyday life.

6.1. The Birth of Culinary Traditions

Tracing the origins of any culinary tradition is akin to navigating a complex evolutionary maze, bound by a multitude of factors such as geography, climate, culture and historical influences. Early culinary methods were practical responses to these conditions. Over time, as techniques were refined and ingredients diversified through trade, exploration, and migration, these methods morphed into expressions of local identity, community culture, and even societal status.

It began simply with the discovery of fire, altering the way our ancestors consumed food. Cooking made food safer and easier to digest, permitting a diversified diet. The advent of agriculture was another milestone, expanding the dietary repertoire with cereals, pulses and, later, spices. The development of preservation techniques, such as curing, pickling, and smoking opened up new possibilities for seasoning and texture, enriching culinary art even further.

6.2. Cuisine as a Cultural Tapestry

Food preferences, rituals and techniques are often deeply entrenched in societal norms and customs. Every community has unique food taboos and delights, shaped by religious beliefs, superstitions and the ecosystem. These elements, when interwoven, form the foundation of cultural identities expressed through food.

In countries such as China or Italy, food isn't simply sustenance; it's a form of communal bonding and an integral element of celebrations. Such communal experiences are influenced by the natural environment, from coastal regions where seafood dominates the palate, to arid landscapes where nomadic tribes developed preservation techniques for dairy and meat. Every meal communicates something profound about the people behind it.

6.3. The Culinary Evolution: A Tale of East Meets West

Trade routes, political alliances, and colonial conquests have dramatically influenced global cuisine. Be it the introduction of chillies to India through Portuguese merchants or the global popularity of pasta due to Italy's geographical affinity to wheat cultivation; these instances underline how food transcends borders, influencing and being influenced by the world.

The Silk Road is a brilliant example of culinary globalisation. This ancient trade route comprising land and maritime paths facilitated the exchange of products, culinary styles and food preservation techniques across diverse cultures. It led to the introduction of ingredients like Persian spinach to China, Chinese peaches to Rome, and Central Asian horse milk to Mongolia.

6.4. A Taste of the Continents: Unpacking Global Flavors

In the spirit of a true culinary exploration, let's embark on a four-course journey across the continents, savoring the best they have to offer.

The "Appetizer" takes us to Asia, the origin of rice cultivation and fermentation techniques that have influenced pickles, kimchi, and even beer.

The "First Course" leads to the rustic kitchens of Africa, boasting hearty stews and the buzz of Moroccan spice markets with their distinct sweet and tangy flavors.

During the "Main Course", European cuisine unfolds its rich tapestry from the hearty shepherd's pie of the British Isles to the exquisite grape wines of France's vineyards.

Finally, for "Dessert", the Americas greet us with varied delicacies, from the vanilla orchids of Mexico, the raisin-studded panettone of Italian-American communities, to Canadian maple syrup.

6.5. A Lavish Affair: Feasts and Festivities

Feasts are the mirror of a society; they elucidate cultural disparities and share historical events. The Thanksgiving turkey symbolizes gratitude, while the Chinese Spring Festival feast brings together families, signifying harmony and prosperity. The Scandinavian smorgasbord celebrates the bounty of the sea, while South Indian feasts, served on banana leaves, symbolize a close connection to the earth.

6.6. Responsibly Savoring Our Gastronomic Heritage

In an age of rapid globalization, culinary traditions are under threat as global food chains homogenize our diets. We must consciously strive to appreciate, conserve, and sustain our culinary heritage. Food tourism, cooking traditional recipes, and engaging with local food economies are excellent ways to begin.

As we reach the end of this gastronomic journey, remember, every morsel savored is part of a well-seasoned narrative from the leaves of our collective past. Let us cherish these culinary traditions, for they are the flavorful mosaics that bring coloor and aroma to the grand painting of our shared cultural heritage. And so, every bite becomes a gateway that lets us taste the vast richness of our shared human experience.

Chapter 7. Dressing the Part: The Role of Traditional Attire

The rich tapestry of our shared history comes alive in every stitch and seam of traditional attire. It not only presents a visual manifestation of our diverse cultural expressions but also tells a poignant narrative of our past, embodying generations of ritual, folklore, labor, and celebration.

7.1. The Evolution of Traditional Dress

Over centuries, fashion has been a vibrant form of human expression, weaving together aesthetics, rituals, societal norms, and geographical environments. The evolution of traditional dress is an illuminating journey, tracing the contours of human migration, trade, climate, and cultural influences. From the coarse wool garments of medieval Europe to the silk Kimonos of feudal Japan, the evolution of traditional attire echoes the rise and fall of civilizations, the exchange of ideas, and the intricacy of human life through the ages.

The first garments worn by our prehistoric ancestors were dictated more by necessity than fashion. Early humans wrapped themselves in the skins of slain animals, giving rise to the first primitive forms of clothing. As centuries passed, humans began to sew these pieces together, creating more complex outfits catering to their needs. Animal skins gradually gave way to plant fibers as better tools and techniques evolved, millennia later giving birth to weaving and knitting.

From the frigid tundras of the Arctic to the scorching deserts of North Africa, geography has played a pivotal role in shaping traditional attire. From the use of deer hide by Native American tribes to the flowing, breathable garments of the Tuareg people of the Sahara, the environment has continually dictated the materials and styles employed in traditional dress.

7.2. Symbols and Storytelling in Traditional Attire

Traditional attire is more than a simple means of covering one's body; it's a storyteller, an identity marker, and a coding of beliefs, conventions, and histories. In many cultures worldwide, traditional attire carries intricate symbolism and meaning, encoded in colors, patterns, embroidery, and design, each unique to its specific cultural context.

In Ghana, for example, the Kente cloth, worn on special occasions, is an expression of history, philosophy, ethics, oral literature, moral values, social code of conduct, religious beliefs, and aesthetic principles. Each color and pattern used in the cloth has a specific meaning, creating a complex language of visual symbolism that is understood and appreciated by the community.

Likewise, in the Maori culture of New Zealand, flax woven cloaks (or Korowai) are much more than mere clothing. The intricate patterns and details indicate the rank of the wearer within their tribe, while the intricacy and age of the cloak itself can hint at the person's lineage and heritage.

7.3. The Role of Dress in Ritual and Celebration

Celebration and ceremony have always been central pillars of human society, and traditional attire has always played a significant role in these. From wedding saris in India to the hanbok worn on Korean birthdays, these garments lend a touch of sacredness and nostalgia to life's milestones. Whether signifying the transition from childhood to adulthood, marrying, or marking the end of the harvest season, traditional attire often plays a pivotal role, binding people to their ancestral roots and tethering the continuity of cultural expressions.

Among the Plains Indian tribes of North America, eagle feathers are worn on special occasions to denote strength and bravery in battle. In Japan, the ornate patterned kimonos, known as Uchikake, are symbolic of prosperity and happiness, worn by brides during traditional wedding ceremonies.

Moreover, festivals remain a time-honored tradition where traditional clothing is brought out in all its glory. Whether it's the vivid and ornate costumes adorned for Carnival in Brazil, the flamenco dresses worn during Feria de Abril in Seville, Spain, or the gorgeously decorated Mardi Gras Indian suits in New Orleans, Louisiana, these celebratory occasions paint a vibrant tableau of our shared human heritage.

7.4. Preserving and Reimagining Traditional Attire

As the world globalizes and cultures blend, preserving traditional dress is critical in maintaining a connection with our roots. However, preservation does not mean stagnation. Designers across the globe are reinterpreting traditional attire, infusing classic styles with a modern sensibility. These modern interpretations of traditional fashion underscore the dynamic, living essence of culture while respecting and preserving its integral values.

Yet, as we explore and appreciate the variety of traditional attire from cultures around the world, it's crucial to approach with respect and understanding, recognizing the depth of history, identity, and cultural pride embedded in each garment.

In conclusion, traditional attire is a complex and powerful cultural expression, a narrative of mankind's odyssey through the ages, encapsulating a kaleidoscope of human experiences - the struggle, the joy, the celebration, and the belief. Indeed, there is so much more to traditional attire than meets the eye - it's a timeless, evolving communication that forms the warp and weft of our shared human heritage.

Chapter 8. The Traditions of Storytelling and Oral Histories

Stepping onto the trail of the timeless yesteryears, we embark on a journey to uncover the rich tapestry of storytelling and oral histories. This voyage is akin to entering a corridor of meandering tales, where each word uttered echoes the vivid realities and expansive imaginations of our ancestors.

8.1. The Origins of Storytelling and Oral Histories

Storytelling, a tradition as ancient as humanity itself, has been an integral part of our shared experience. The birth of storytelling traces back to the nascent days of human civilization, when our ancestors used primitive languages to share experiences, teach values, and understand the world around them. This practice evolved from simple tales around a campfire, elucidating day-to-day survival, to complex narratives shaping societies and cultures. Storytelling and oral histories have transcended time and space, becoming the sinew linking us to the earliest epochs of human experience.

8.2. The Role and Importance of Oral Histories

Oral history, like a deeply cherished heirloom, has been passed down through generations. It stands as a powerful testament to our collective past, immortalized in the minds of our ancestors, who in turn have echoed these tales through the generations. Oral histories bear witness to civilizations formed and fallen, empires risen and decayed, heroes and villains born and perished, and tales of triumph and despair.

They are more than mere chronicles; they are bridges, spanning the gap between past and present, bringing forth lessons engraved on the slate of time. They provide an intimate view into the past, often offering perspectives not reflected in traditional historical accounts. They contribute to a broader understanding of cultural, social, and political contexts that have shaped humankind.

8.3. Storytelling: A Cultural Staple

In every corner of the world, communities share their unique lore through storytelling. Whether it's the vibrant folktales of the African continent, the captivating epics of ancient Greece, the intricate shadow puppetry of Asia, or the indigenous legends of the Americas, storytelling threads together our shared cultural fabric. Rich and diverse, these narratives affirm our shared human experience, probing the very depths of our values, beliefs, dreams, and fears.

8.4. Methods of Transmission

Narratives have been transferred through numerous mediums. Oral recitation, theater, music, dance, and visual arts are some of the vivid landscapes where these narratives have been sown. Different societies have perfected their unique methods; some rely on the enchanting rhythm of songs while others instill tales in intricate dances or theatrical performances. Regardless of the method, the goal remains the same: to keep the flame of history alive and to pass it on to the next generation.

8.5. Architecture of a Story

Undeniably, crafting a compelling story requires an adept

understanding of its structure. In general, stories are composed of a well-defined beginning, middle, and end, each fulfilling a unique purpose. The beginning sets the stage and introduces the characters. The middle expands the plot, introduces conflicts, and builds suspense. The end brings resolution and offers a moral or a lesson. This structure, while simple in outline, is filled with complexities that breathe life into narratives.

8.6. The Role of the Storyteller

The role of the storyteller extends beyond narrating a sequence of events; they are caretakers of memory, wisdom, and tradition. With nuanced expressions, rhythmic tones, and captivating gestures, storytellers unlock the door to an auditory and sensory experience that allows listeners to plunge into the depths of the narrative world. The storyteller's skill to animate characters and settings makes experiences from the past tangible, making the listener a participant in the tale rather than a mere observer.

8.7. The Modern-Day Relevance of Storytelling and Oral Histories

In this digital age, oral histories and storytelling hold their ground firmly. They continue to serve as powerful tools for education and a source of entertainment. They create a sense of community and shared history and are crucial in preserving and revitalizing endangered languages and cultures. They are also beginning to play a pivotal role in human rights advocacy, where personal stories of oppression and resilience can initiate dialogue and incite change.

Through this exploration of storytelling and oral histories, it becomes evident that they are not merely tales of our ancestors' past. They are indeed whispering echoes of our history, offering invaluable insights into humanity's diversified cultural landscape. From the past's elaborate canvas to the future's unwritten manuscript, storytelling and oral history remain the perpetual narrators, transmitting the legacy of our collective heritage. Like treasure chests, they hold the invaluable gems of time, waiting for an explorer to uncover them and immerse themselves in the timeless echoes of human experience.

Chapter 9. Milestone Celebrations: Festivals and Rituals

The intoxicating scents of food, the rhythmic cadence of music, the exuberant cheers of community members — all encapsulate the vibrant essence of festivals and rituals that play a predominant role in the cultural fabric of societies worldwide. These milestone celebrations act as vehicles for transmission of cultural beliefs and practices, often transcending generations, to link the past, present, and future. They colourfully illustrate tales of ancestry and spirituality, of triumph and recurrence, and of unity and identity, thus serving as a mirror to the society they originate from.

9.1. Unfolding the Meaning of Rituals and Festivals

Rituals and festivals are a prism through which we can view the customs and traditions of various cultures. Rituals, in their broadest sense, involve a series of actions performed to serve a cultural or religious purpose. They provide a structure through which fundamental beliefs and values are reinforced, bolstering our sense of place within the community and the universe itself.

Festivals, on the other hand, tend to be recurring celebrations which may honour a religious event, the changing seasons, or a historical occasion. They often serve as collective expressions of joy, wonder, and reverence, where the whole community comes together to participate in shared customs. These festive occasions often shine a light on the shared history and values of a community, reinforcing a sense of unity and continuity through time.

9.2. An Evolution Through the Ages

Historically, rituals and festivals often evolved from a desire to understand and influence the world. Early humans interpreted natural phenomena through a supernatural lens, giving birth to numerous myths and rituals. Fast-forward to the present day, these ceremonies and celebrations have inevitably changed, some adapting to suit the modern world, and others remaining relatively static, largely retaining their original form. Although the modes of celebrations have transformed dramatically, the essence of constructing a meaningful connectedness within communities and fostering reverence for the perceived divine powers has continually been the central theme.

9.3. Vibrant Expressions of Cultures Worldwide

Across the globe, every culture and society has its own unique set of festivals and rituals. To delve into the details of a few representative ones is to undertake a remarkable exploration of human spirit and socio-cultural idiosyncrasies.

For instance, imagine the effervescent energy of Brazil's 'Carnival', a pre-Lenten festival filled with music, dance, and vibrant costumes. It's a stark contrast to Japan's tranquil 'Obon', a Buddhist event honouring the departed spirits of ancestors, featuring the beautiful custom of floating lanterns on water.

Contrastingly, one encounters sober mysticism in the 'Day of the Dead' in Mexico, a festival that joyously celebrates the cyclical nature of life by commemorating those who have passed on. On another geo-cultural front, the ebullient 'Holi', celebrated in Indian subcontinent, bathes people in myriad hues – a riotous celebration of spring and victory of goodness over evil.

9.4. Intrinsic Lessons of Festivals and Rituals

Rituals and festivals, each with their own distinctive parameters, teach us lessons on humanity, coexistence, and respect for nature and the supernatural. They serve as nodal points for collective memory and societal bonding, for cultural education and continuity, and for marking important life transitions and the passage of seasons.

While it is tempting to perceive these pompous displays as mere spectacles, they carry much deeper implications. They emphasize the power of togetherness, uphold the compelling lore of mythologies, and remind us of the ethos which binds a community together. They are the lifeblood of cultural transmission, creating a vibrant tapestry of human expressions that enrich our global heritage.

9.5. The Cultural Explorer's Journey into the Celebratory Maze

For the cultural explorer, participating in these celebrations or observing them is an enlightening immersion into the ethos of a community. But respect and understanding must guide the exploration. Understanding the core significance of these rituals, their historical and cultural contexts, and their contemporary meanings will ensure an enriching and respectful experience.

It is also important to remember, each festival and ritual echoes the resonant frequencies of our shared human history, spotlighting various dimensions of human experience. By engaging with these milestone celebrations, the cultural explorer can embrace the world's diverse cultures and contribute to the ongoing dialogue surrounding cultural preservation and appreciation.

In sum, festivals and rituals narrate incomparable stories of cultural conception, evolution, and continuity. They are the human race's artistic response to the spiritual and physical phenomena of our world, embodying beliefs, values, and traditions. Through these riveting chapters of social celebration, we learn to appreciate the abundant diversity that adorns our world, and build bridges of understanding and respect that underpin a harmonious global community.

Chapter 10. Understanding Value: The Role of Cultural Artifacts

To explore the profound sphere of cultural artifacts, we ought to remember that they are not just objects but resilient remnants of our ancestors' lives, bearers of knowledge, and the connective threads that stitch together the narrative of our collective past. These artifacts narrate tales of our cultural evolution, imbued with symbolism and suffused with rich historical narratives that resonate with shared human experiences.

10.1. The Concept of Value in Cultural Artifacts

The term "value" carries multiple connotations that revolve around not just economic or aesthetic standing but also intrinsic significance. Cultural artifacts encompass all the elements that make us human – our beliefs, our myths, our rituals, and our social structures. They are instrumental in providing us with an authentic understanding of the past, which informs our present situation and guides our future trajectory. It's essential to realize that the "value" of an artifact doesn't lie solely in its material worth but in its capability to detail histories, construct identities and forge connections.

10.2. Narrating Histories, Constructing Identities

Cultural artifacts are fundamental in documenting human progress over the millennia. From the cave paintings of prehistoric times that express mankind's earliest artistic inclinations to technological artifacts like the ancient Antikythera mechanism that reveal the advanced knowledge of past civilizations, these items bear witness to our species' persistent march through time. Simultaneously, they also construct identities by revealing specific cultural practices and imprints. For instance, hieroglyphs on Egyptian tomb walls provide insights into their social structures, religious beliefs, and understanding of mortality, thereby enabling us to construct a more accurate image of ancient Egyptian civilization.

10.3. Artifacts: Linking the Past to the Future

Artifacts are mediums that link the past to the present, extending a bridge to the future. They stimulate scholarly inquiry, inspire creative imagination, and stoke public fascination. When curated and displayed in museums or other spaces and even viewed online, these artifacts not only present the achievements of humanity but also provoke philosophical contemplation. Considering their significance, artefacts often serve as focal points during cultural revitalization efforts, enabling societies to regain their sense of identity and heritage during crucial times of change or adaptation.

10.4. Preservation and the Consequences of Lost Artifacts

The preservation of cultural artifacts is critical, and the loss or destruction of these irreplaceable treasures is a loss to our collective human heritage. Whether through natural disaster, war, negligence, or illegal trafficking, the loss of artifacts signifies the extinguishing of diverse narratives and the erasure of human histories. Consequently, numerous international bodies and local institutions are engaged in the active preservation, recovery, and restitution of these valuable objects.

10.5. Interacting with Artifacts Responsibly: A Duty for Citizens of the World

Responsible engagement with cultural artifacts isn't just for historians, archaeologists, or curators. It's a shared duty for all global citizenship. To value an artifact is to respect its originating culture. It includes supporting preservation efforts, behaving responsibly when interacting with artifacts, and assisting in combatting illicit trafficking.

An artifact is a window into the complex panorama of human history and cultural interplay. As we explore their stories, we learn not just about those who made them, but, by extension, about ourselves and the myriad of human traditions scattered across the globe. We, as citizens of the world, must understand that the true value of cultural artifacts transcends beyond the tangible; it nestles within the intelligence, creativity, and endurance of human experience, threaded through all walks of life.

Concluding this deep dive into the world of cultural artifacts, one is left with a profound appreciation for the depth of human endeavor and understanding. Let these token remnants of humanity, so brimming with history, wisdom, and cultural significance, serve as your compass; a means of navigating the labyrinthine pathways of human existence, reminding us of our shared past as we continue to weave the tapestry of human civilization into an ever-evolving design. The role of cultural artifacts isn't merely to be finders of lost time, but as guides aiding us as we journey onward, armed with a deeper comprehension of who we are, where we have been, and where we might one day dream to venture.

In the end, understanding value in terms of cultural artifacts isn't about collecting objets d'art or aesthetic appreciation alone. It's about grasping the threads of continuity and embracing the tapestry of human heritage that leads to a broader, richer perspective on our world, our past, and our shared experiences. The real value, then, lies in our capacity to learn from and cherish these cultural artifacts, these glimpses of past civilizations that have indeed crafted our present. They encourage us to question, to explore, and ultimately, to understand a bit more about the intricate and diverse planet we call home.

Chapter 11. The Modern-day Cultural Explorer: Engaging with Heritage Responsibly

For the informed, responsible, and discerning modern day cultural explorer, reaching into the annals of our shared human past is no mere leisure pursuit. It's an act dissecting the vibrant multiverse of cultures, understanding one's relationship with it, and engaging in a respectful symbiosis with the shared world heritage.

11.1. Building Knowledge: Essential Reading and Research

Expanding one's knowledge in a thorough way nurtures curiosity, deepens understanding and helps develop informed perspectives. For the cultural explorer, researching about various cultures, traditions, and practices around the world is a significant first step. This involves delving into books, articles, documentaries, and credible online resources to develop nuanced understanding. Credible academic papers, anthropology and sociology research works, biographies, cultural documentaries and platforms like the UNESCO World Heritage site are excellent sources for enriching knowledge.

By leveraging these resources, a cultural explorer can gain context about historical timelines, cultural nuances, and subtle interplay of socio-economic factors that molded civilizations. Importantly, obtaining knowledge about the historical conflicts and their subsequent impact is crucial to avoid potential cultural insensitivity and misinterpretation.

11.2. Sensitivity Brings Insight: Respecting Sociocultural Sensibilities and Taboos

One must be mindful of understanding and honoring cultural nuances, traditions, values, and taboos that shape each community and culture. Each culture carries with it an intricate web of sociocultural sensibilities, some visible, others underlying. Therefore, learning about cultural practices, traditions, symbols and their meanings can save a cultural explorer from committing cultural faux pas. This cultural sensitivity will also open unseen doors, enable authentic engagements, and inspire genuine respect from the inhabitants of the culture being explored.

This involves learning the local etiquette, understanding accepted social conduct, respecting religious sites and ceremonies, acknowledging the weight of historical artifacts and ensuring interactions with local communities are polite and respectful. The principle of respect also extends to our environment. Thus, being respectful towards natural landscapes, conserving biodiversity, minimizing waste, and reducing one's carbon footprint are also elemental for all cultural explorers.

11.3. Participate, Don't Appropriate: Engaging with Cultural Practices Mindfully

Cultural engagement is more meaningful when one avoids mere "cultural tourism" and instead actively participates within the framework of respect and understanding. Engaging in the local way of life, participating in cultural ceremonies, trying out traditional cuisine, clothing or dance forms, can all add depth to the journey of cultural exploration.

However, participating should not transgress into cultural appropriation. Cultural symbols, clothing, rituals or languages are not merely exotic 'elements' to be cherry picked, rather these bear deep emotional, historical and symbolic significance for the indigenous communities. So, when participating, one must be aware and sensitive not to appropriate, misrepresent, disrespect or trivialize the cultural uniqueness for personal amusement or benefit.

11.4. The Ethical Explorer: Responsible Consumption and Support for Local Artisans and Industries

One of the ways in which a modern cultural explorer can responsibly interact with the heritage is through mindful consumer behavior. Being an ethical consumer involves purchasing authentic crafts, traditional artisanal goods, locally produced food and drink, and more. This not only supports the local economy and artisans but also helps preserve traditional crafts and methods of production.

At a broader level, this can also involve supporting community-based cultural experiences such as home-stays, local culinary experiences, guided community tours, and local festivals. These authentic interactions create an enriching exchange between visitors and residents, supporting local communities and contributing to the safeguarding and promotion of cultural heritage.

11.5. The Heritage Promoter: Advocating and Protecting Cultural Heritage

As cultural explorers, we ought to be guardians and advocates of the rich, varied, and colourful heritage of our world. This involves actively promoting responsible cultural engagement, respectful behaviour, and the importance of preserving cultural heritage. As engaged explorers, we can raise awareness, support preservation initiatives, and rally against actions that threaten to dilute, destroy, or misrepresent cultural heritage.

We are at a unique vantage point in human history, where the tools of information, insight, and influence are within our reach. This is a calling for us to collectively heighten our consciousness and face our profound responsibility to protect, promote and engage with our shared global cultural heritage mindfully, responsibly, and respectfully. The journey as a modern day cultural explorer is a journey of discovery, wonder, enlightenment, and respectful symbiosis with our world heritage. So, embark on this enriching journey, understand the past, comprehend its influence on the present, and responsibly contribute to nurturing our shared cultural heritage for the future generations.